SometimesThe Wind Blows Sideways: Our Lives with a Special Needs Child

Stories Compiled by:

Amy Quonce

WindingRoadBook.Weebly.Com

CONTENTS

ACKNOWLEDGMENTS

First and foremost, I would like to thank all of the families who had the courage to submit such personal stories to share with the world.

For my writing accountability partner Lisa Buske, who provided me with valuable insights and support. It is because of your encouragement that I continued to write.

To Mary Buske, who did a wonderful job on the photos that became my book cover.

To all my friends and family who have supported me in my ventures, Thank You!

I would like to thank my daughter Elizabeth for always trying her very best each and every day. Your determination and loving disposition has always been the inspiration for all of my writing.

Last, but not least, I need to thank my husband Dan for giving up so much time with me so that I could work on my writing. I love you!

INTRODUCTION

Having a child with disabilities isn't something that anybody plans on, yet each year thousands of people are faced with just that. They are thrown into something that they are unprepared for, and it can leave families feeling secluded and worried about the uncertainty of their future. Fifteen years ago I found myself among those who have struggled to come to terms with exactly what this label would mean to them.

For me, denial was my first reaction when I was told that my daughter had disabilities. As much as I didn't want to face the reality, watching her lack of progress forced me to move beyond my image of what I wanted life to be like for her. As a parent, you feel responsible for teaching your child what they need to know in life, but when your child fails to achieve these milestones, you take it personally and wonder what you did wrong. I've learned that the answer to that question is simple… nothing.

We as parents need to step back and instead of thinking, "Why did I fail my child?", we need to think, "How can I better help my child?" This may mean accepting help from outside of the family unit, which for me was the hardest part. I secretly hated that my world now revolved around a constant schedule of therapists and doctor appointments. It was overwhelming, and I knew of nobody else that could even remotely relate to my situation.

Learning how to care for a child with special needs was a very unique process. There is no literature out there that tells you what will work for your child, so I made it up as I went along. If something worked, I went with it no matter how unconventional it was. You learn how to get creative when your child is afraid of the most simple things in life such as food, soap or even Play-Doh. This is when I really started to value the expertise of my daughter's therapists. It was hard work, but the lessons that she learned were invaluable and I quickly realized that she may not have survived without them.

Eventually, I got involved with some of the wonderful programs in Oswego County such as ARISE and Parents of Special Children, which connected me with other families in similar situations. I began to see that we were not so different than what I had thought years ago. I got to know a lot of very nice people who all wanted the same thing in this world: More acceptance from society.

Knowing that I am my daughter's best friend is very hard on me. She has been lucky enough where people generally are nice to her, but that is as far as it goes. There are no birthday party invites, no sleepovers, no hanging out with her friends. Her world consists solely of what I create for her.

Socialization is probably one of the hardest concepts that developmentally disabled children face. They may not know how to carry on a conversation or play in the typical way as other kids do, but they do know when they are being singled out or being made fun of.

Being the parent or caregiver of a person with a disability is no doubt the toughest and most rewarding job that anybody can have. It takes a lot of hard work, patience and dedication, but the rewards that you get in return are priceless. These children are among the most loving, innocent and sweetest people that have ever graced this Earth. They love unconditionally and ask for almost nothing in return, and I am grateful that I was one of the chosen ones to have a special needs child in my life.

I hope that the stories in this book will comfort your heart, heal your pain, and induce a smile into your day. May you never feel alone in your journey.

~Amy Quonce

This story was slightly modified from it's original print in the Arise monthly newsletter, March 2011.

Someone's daughter or son, treat them right
Opportunist
Motivated and driven by desire and a will to succeed
Enlightened before their time, recognize life will not always
be easy
Tested on a daily bases -- whether it be at home, school,
work or in public
Ingenious problem solving techniques
Manage to find every loop hole to maximize their learning
Entertaining – they enjoy making others smile
Simply...MARVELOUS!

Talented in areas outside the classroom
Hearts to love without limitation
Energetic and motivated

Willing to learn differently
Individuals with a heart for others
Notoriously gifted and special
Dare to be different, in a good way

Brilliant, yet struggle to express this to others
Loyal, loving, and true
Outside of the box thinkers, thank goodness
Whimsical, fun and creative
Similar to their peers when given the opportunity to show it

Scholars in their own right
Interested in new ways to learn
Dedicated to the task at hand
Eager to be the best they can
Willing to help others who struggle because they understand how it feels
Always there for a friend
Young and youthful, regardless of their age
Sincere with their apologies and words

Lisa M. Buske

A writer and speaker, Lisa is a catalyst for others affected by tragedy. Her sister's abduction in 1994 left her depressed and lonely yet with God's hand at work in her heart and life...true healing took place. Through her writing and speaking she engages the audience while sharing her heart to help others in their personal journeys. She writes a column, "Through our eyes...", that appears in the National Center for Missing & Exploited Children's: Ride for Missing Children monthly bulletin, has been a contributing writer for local newspapers, and has presented workshops for both educators and college students. In addition, she maintains a website and blog: http://lisabuske.weebly.com. For more information about Lisa or to follow her blog, visit her website today.

In addition to writing, Lisa works as a teacher's assistant with the Mexico Academy & Central School district, is active with various church ministries, and devotes time to her family and friends.

Writing for Him. to keep Heidi's memory alive with prayers to heal those affected by abduction.

The Value of Life

As I sat in the doctor's office listening to him tell me that my baby would have no quality of life and that I should consider an abortion, a million things were running through my head. *Why me? What did I do wrong? Will my life ever be the same?* But never once did it occur to me to follow through on the well meaning advice of a doctor who didn't have a clue. I was going to have this baby, and I would provide her with the best life possible.

What that meant I wasn't really sure of at the time. Never having had any contact with a person who had a disability, I was oblivious as to what to expect or how to even go about getting the care my newborn would require. So I simply took it, one day at a time, and I allowed her to be my guide.

The day she entered into this world I looked down into the eyes of my flawless looking daughter and named her Elizabeth. I vowed to her that I was going to try my best, if she would only be patient with me. And so we ventured on a journey full of ups and downs. For every step back we took, Elizabeth found a way to make my heart grow just a little bit larger. Her loving disposition and innocent looking face made every trip to the doctors worthwhile. She was the sweetest little girl I had ever put my eyes on, but at the age of 5 we still had no concrete name for what we were dealing with. No label, no statistics, no research that would tell us what to expect in the future. A little bit of this and a touch of that never meshed together for a real diagnosis. So I have decided to call this no name anomaly 'Innocent Syndrome'; for that's what it truly reflects- a child who was innocent in every aspect of her life.

It was hard as a mother to watch my child struggle so much in life. When she entered Kindergarten she was still not talking, and seemed to only gravitate towards adults, without even giving her peers a second thought. Worried about her becoming the scapegoat for cruel childhood teasing, I tried to overcompensate by making sure she had the finest of clothing and the latest trends in order to appear as typical as possible. I didn't want her viewed as 'different'. But Elizabeth didn't care. She was happy in her own little world. Stacking books and sorting cards out seemed like much more fun to her than going to somebody's house to play with dolls. But still I worried.

As her body grew rapidly, her brain seemed to develop at a much slower rate. By the time she reached her teenage years she looked no different than her classmates on the outside, yet inside there was still this innocent little girl peeking through.

The countless hours she spent with her books and cards were much more intense for her, and while now very verbal, she still only wanted to `chit chat` with the grown ups. Would I ever be able to get her to fit in?

But as I sat back and observed she was fitting in… in her own way. She had made herself friends within the community without my even realizing it. Everywhere we went, Elizabeth would find an adult that she would deem her buddy and spend countless hours filling them in on her life. And they would listen. Over and over they joked with her over who was sillier, smiled in surprise as she once again announced how old she was, and graciously accepted hugs whenever they were offered. The waitresses, cashiers, and receptionists were all her posse, and she loved it. She had found her own way to find a place in this world and it didn't involve fancy clothes or expensive gadgets. The only thing she ever wanted was acceptance, and she found it by being herself.

My daughter may not have straight A's, friends over on the weekends, or even a name for this thing that has changed our lives forever. But what she does possess is something greater. With a carefree attitude and an unconditional love for everything and everyone, she has the quality of life that few others have. I often think back to that doctor and wonder why he felt that her life was of no value, when all along she held the key to happiness within her heart.

And so the girl that I thought I would have to teach everything to has taught me the one lesson in life that I will treasure forever. Being yourself is the best thing of all.

Amy Quonce

Amy Quonce works in special education at the Oswego City School District. She lives with her husband and daughter and enjoys spending her free time walking the shorelines of beautiful Lake Ontario.

Currently, Amy is working on the final edits of her first true life novel which she plans on publishing soon. Please visit her website at WindingRoadBook.Weebly.Com, or email her at WindingRoadBook@aol.com.

Molliemae's Heart

My niece, Molliemae, is a three year old Down's child. She is bit small for her age because she was born with a defective heart and they had to wait until she was six months old to operate and fix it. She didn't do much growing in those first six months of her life because her heart was so weak.

I don't get to spend much time with her. When I do see her I normally have to chase her down, scoop her up in my arms and steal a kiss, and if I am lucky, she might give me a hug, too. She is just far too busy a girl for all that mushy stuff!

This past July one of my sisters lost her oldest son in an accident. Molliemae was at the funeral with us all and after the service I saw her in the arms of another family member, so I went over to her and gave her a big kiss on the cheek. She smiled that big, beautiful smile of hers and then promptly reached her little arm out to me, grabbed me around the neck and pulled me to her in a big, tight hug.

Needless to say, I was very surprised and touched beyond words. She has never spontaneously hugged me (and never has since). It's like she instinctively knew that particular day how sad I was and how badly I needed that little bit of love from her. I had hugged a whole lot of people during the two days we had all spent in that funeral home but none of those hugs comforted me or moved me as much as the one I got from our little Molliemae on that sad day. I will never forget that special moment with that special little girl and how much it meant to me to receive such a random act of kindness and love from a little girl who obviously has such a big, strong heart.

I think that heart doctor of hers fixed her up just fine. Maybe he even put a little something extra in there for her to share with us all. Something beautiful and pure, warm and fuzzy. something to fill our own hearts with so we don't have to be so sad even in the worst of times.

Terri Adrian

Terri Adrian lives in Oswego, NY. She has a BFA in Art from SUNY Oswego and works as a Reike Therapist. She is the mother of one grown son, Lucas. She enjoys making art, spending time with her family, reading, gardening, photography and writing poetry. She is a spiritualist who enjoys dabbling in the paranormal and working with nature energies. She dislikes winter and loves October. If you would like to contact her, she can be reached at moonflower316@hotmail.com.

Actions Speak Louder Than Words

The other day I caught bits and pieces of the funeral coverage on CNN for Senator Edward Kennedy. I remember the deaths of JFK and Bobby so it seemed appropriate that I should see at least some of this funeral. It was moving in many ways, intriguing to think how many people felt the need to remember and touch some part of this, the Kennedy legacy. Why is this man, this family so enthralling? Why are we drawn, by some unseen force, to want to be like them or at the very least get near them? I'm not sure that we'll ever really know but I am more drawn now than ever, that is after hearing Teddy Kennedy Jr. eulogize his father. It was a moment that will remain with me for a very long time.

Teddy told of a time, only two short months after losing his leg to bone cancer at the age of 12 when he recalled his father coming home from his work as a senator on the hill in Washington. It was a snowy wintry day. His father it seemed dug around the garage until he could find a sled and then beckoned for his still-recovering son to join him in some sledding. To a 12 year old boy sledding is second nature, but to a 12 year old boy just learning to navigate on a prosthetic leg it proved to be very difficult. The younger Kennedy struggled on the snowy slope, falling several times until breaking down in tears and telling his father that he couldn't do it; he would NEVER be able to do it. This is when Teddy Jr., in a broken voice, recalled his father lifting him into his strong fatherly arms and telling his little man that he COULD do it; he could do anything. Then the senior Kennedy told his son that it didn't matter if it took all day but TOGETHER they would climb that hill and TOGETHER they would beat that slope and that is what they did. There are pictures of a smiling man and boy stacked like cord wood on a single sled flying fearless down a snowy slope with not a care in the world. It looked as if their only thought was the pure joy of being free and unrestrained by disability or fear.

I cried a bit when I heard that; as I have a tear or two welling up while writing about it. It was a very emotional story and it hit my heart like a rocket. How will my kids eulogize me? I have no doubt that I will never be a senator or a lawyer or a major mover or shaker in our society. I don't really want to be any of those. What I do want is for my kids to need me and rely on me and remember me as the one who told them that they could do anything, **then showed them how**. I think that I am missing that a bit; I am getting bogged down in little details and forgetting the big lesson. I'm here every minute for my kids, but is cooking their meals being there for them? Is creating elaborate social stories for my son really, really being there for him? I think, perhaps, my daughter would rather I throw together a quick sandwich so that she and I can finish reading that book together. Perhaps my son would benefit more from a social story if I made a point to act out the parts with him some night instead of quickly reading it and then passing it on to school. It's not just important to let them know they have the power to succeed but they need to KNOW that we are there every step of the way to show them what success really looks like. I gotta go - my son is in the pool and he is trying so very hard to get on that raft. I think it's time I got wet!

Karen Delaney

Karen Delaney lives in Oswego, New York with her husband, Dan and 14 year old twins, Adam and Erin. Karen started her working career as a registered nurse but since her son's autism diagnosis 12 years ago she has spent the majority of her days working with her son, advocating for him and others on the spectrum and trying to ensure a typical childhood for his sister. Karen enjoys being with her family, remodeling their home, gardening and working with technology. She is active in several organizations such as the Oswego County Autism Task Force and OPT IN (Oswego Parent/Teacher Inclusion Network) where Karen enjoys creating web site content, letter writing campaigns to the media and legislators as well as keeping the financial records. To contact Karen you can e-mail her at k.delaney@twcny.rr.com.

Unforeseen Journey

My Name is Melanie Coleman. I'm 36-years old, and I want to share my story about a special little guy that happened into our lives. I can't remember a time when I didn't want a family. I was hoping for a little later in life, but to my husband's and my surprise, on July 21, 1995 our journey began. Tyler John came into the world right on time with my due date, weighing 7lbs 6oz. He was 22 inches long, with ten fingers, ten toes. It was such a happy day! Little did we know there was a nasty storm brewing inside our perfect little bundle of joy!

Never in a million years did Gary and I see what was coming. When Tyler was six months old he sat up on his own, and that was the end of his milestones. Gary and I did have a couple little signs, now looking back. Tyler had a large forehead and his right eye was a little outward. I took Tyler to the doctor with my concerns, and was reassured that everything was fine, all babies do things in their own time, so we went on our way. Six months later there was still no cruising along the furniture, no walking, back to the doctor we went. The doctor said his legs were weak and he needed to drink "more milk." I thought about this for two weeks, and decided we needed a second opinion. We found a wonderful pediatrician who also happened to be a neurologist, and she ordered a CT scan of the brain and blood work. She called me the next day to let me know Tyler had what they call hydrocephalus (water on the brain), and we needed to see a neurosurgeon. We found an amazing surgeon who informed us that Tyler also had an arachnoid cyst which was the size of an orange at the base of his brain: A genetic defect caused when CSF (cerebrospinal fluid) rushes into ruptured arachnoid mater. The resulting cyst can then block the normal flow of CSF from the brain, resulting in hydrocephalus as well as other defects. The most common locations for an arachnoid cyst are the middle fossa and the posterior fossa. The most common symptoms are nausea and vertigo.

I do believe the world stopped in that moment in the doctor's office for me, Gary, and my mother. Surgery was scheduled for three weeks later. The surgeon removed most of the cyst, but since it was very close to the eye he had to leave the base of the cyst there. Also, the shunt was placed but not connected. At the time there was a new procedure called an endoscopic third ventriculoscopy, which would have eliminated the need for a shunt, but unfortunately for Tyler it did not work. We tried for three weeks, but fluid kept building up into the top of his head. We went weekly to have the fluid drained off, which was excruciating for him, and devastating for my mother and I, who had to hold him while he screamed to keep him from moving as the doctor inserted a long needle into his skull and drew out the fluid. We'd watch Tyler hopefully after each appointment, praying the fluid wouldn't return, but it always did. The surgeon then preformed the procedure to connect the shunt. We've been very lucky that we have never had a malfunction.

Tyler went home three days after the surgery. We had been home for about three hours when we noticed Tyler was not looking right, very rosy cheeks, and staring off. I called our surgeon's associate, because unfortunately our surgeon was away for two weeks for National Guard duty. I explained to him what was going on with Tyler, and he told me he had just had brain surgery and that I was being a neurotic mother. I hung up and laid Tyler down for bedtime, checked on him about thirty minutes later, and he was in a full blown seizure. Eleven days of ups and downs in the ICU, and we got our boy up and moving and home. Several months of PT and he was finally walking at 19 months. They were the greatest moments, seeing him finally cruising and taking steps!

I wanted to start at the beginning of Tyler's story in hopes that someone going through this and unsure, may find it helpful for them, and especially for their child. If parents make the decision to use a practice with more than one doctor, they must insist on seeing the same doctor for every visit, to allow that doctor to become familiar with their child, who may notice even the smallest of changes in the child. A mistake on my part, being only 20 years old and a new mom, was allowing Tyler to be seen by a different doctor for all four of his well-baby visits. I do believe some of Tyler's damage could have been prevented if a diagnosis had been made sooner.

Tyler not only had the two brain surgeries, but also hernia surgery and corrective eye surgery, then when he was six his appendix ruptured, requiring an appendectomy. I'm totally amazed with Tyler and his strength. Tyler said he had a belly ache, and at about one o'clock in the afternoon let out a spine-tingling scream. After that he said he still had just a belly ache, so we had him lay down for a bit. Something told me we needed to go to the ER, and off we went. We lived in a very small town with a very small hospital, and the ER doctor said Tyler was a very sick young man, his white blood cells were very high, and we needed to transfer him to a bigger hospital, which we did.

Once we got there they couldn't figure out what was wrong with him, because he wasn't acting like he was in that much pain. They took an x-ray of his abdomen and saw some air, but it wasn't telling the story. He had a CT scan, and finally a surgeon who does most of the appendix surgeries looked at the CT, and determined for certain that Tyler had a ruptured appendix. Twenty-four hours later Tyler was in surgery. We were in the hospital for eleven days, and in that time he had two surgeries. The shunt had to be pulled out of his abdomen while his belly healed, and they had to watch the color of the CFS fluid to make sure infection didn't go up through the shunt tube into his brain. I wanted to share this, because I can't remember Tyler crying or complaining of pain, he just took it in stride and dealt with it. Kids are so totally amazing; they just persevere no matter what cards they are dealt.

We now have a very loving, talkative, interesting, stubborn teenager in our lives. Tyler is so happy no matter what. It amazes me to think what he has been through, and what he continues to go through on a daily basis, with no short-term memory and several areas of the brain having been damaged by the fluid. Learning is very difficult for Tyler, but he's up every morning on his own and out the door. He goes to school every day with that amazing smile. Tyler loves music of all kinds, from rap to the oldies. He loves art, especially painting. Did I mention talking? He loves his grandparents. We couldn't have asked for a better support system than we have in our families. If adults who think life is hard could see the world through the eyes of a person with special needs, this world would be a happier, gentler, more patient and loving place.

The message I'm hoping people take away from our story is that parents have to advocate for their children. Even if things seem normal on the outside, if you feel something is going on, push. Doctors are not always right just because they are doctors. Ask questions until you are satisfied. Get a second opinion, a good doctor will welcome a second opinion. In our case Ty really doesn't have a "label". With a brain injury such as his there are no guidelines, we're kind of just winging it, so be reassured that you are doing the best job you know how to do and carry on.

Melanie Coleman

Melanie Coleman has been happily married for 17 years and is the mother of three active boys. She enjoys camping, traveling listening to music and anything the boys may be doing at the time. Melanie is a huge animal lover. The family has several cats and dogs. Sid may be the favorite; he is a little six lb. long haired Chihuahua. Another passion she just found in her life is taking care of the elderly. So very rewarding! Her biggest goal in life is to raise three up standing men. She can be reached at benkey711@yahoo.com.

David's Story

The phone was ringing as we put the key in the lock at our hotel in Glenwood Springs, Colorado. It was my son, Ric, calling to tell us of the birth of their first child.

I hurried to the phone and asked the typical questions a grandmother asks and my son responded "We have a baby boy and we've named him David Francis." He weighed in at five pounds, fourteen ounces. I asked how mother and son were doing and that is when I learned David was born with Down Syndrome. I started to cry and I couldn't stop.

David is in the ICU in an incubator. An apparatus resembling a cake container top is placed over his head to give him the life-saving oxygen he needs. He is hooked up to a heart monitor which emits a loud sound if his heart stops beating. He is too weak to nurse or to suck from a tiny bottle resembling a doll's bottle. He must be fed through a tube inserted into his mouth which leads to his stomach.

Lori goes to the hospital each morning. She suits up in sterile clothing and eagerly enters the area where David lies in his little bed. She strokes David lovingly. When Ric comes in after work, the nurse allows them to take him out of the incubator to hold him for a couple of minutes while the nurse hovers above holding the oxygen to his face.

Five weeks later, David comes home along with an oxygen tank and heart monitor. Once home, he begins to thrive and gain weight. Therapists come twice a week to work on building muscle tone and balance. At age two, he attends Main Street School in North Syracuse where they have an Adaptive Physical Education Program.

From the time of his birth, he responded to music. If he was having trouble settling down for the night, singing softly in his ear would quiet him. As he grew older, he enjoyed listening to music. He received a karaoke machine one Christmas and he loved putting on a top hat and while wielding a cane proceeded to perform for his audience. He is a natural entertainer. From the time he could crawl up on the piano bench at our home, he would "play" the piano. The music on the piano is no longer upside down. The piano light is turned on and David softly and deliberately plays as he moves his body as if he were a concert pianist.

Once David entered Middle School, he was in the school's musicals. His dance partner, Tatiana, also was born with Down Syndrome. Michael, his younger brother, was off stage helping him with costume changes and stage entrances. At the end of the play, students and faculty alike give David thumbs up and tell him what a great job he did.

A tradition we have at Thanksgiving is to go around the table and express what we are thankful for. One year I decided to do things differently. I asked each person to say what they were thankful for about the person sitting to their right. Ric was sitting next to David and he said, "David makes me laugh every day."

He has a fine sense of humor. One Christmas as we are unwrapping gifts, I leave my chair for a moment only to return and see that David has placed something under a cushion of my chair. He laughs hysterically as I sit down on the "whoopi" pad he has placed there!

Shooting hoops is one of David's favorite pastimes and when Dad and Michael join him, it's even better. He's dressed in cargo shorts and a tee shirt. His shoe laces may be untied and sometimes his shoes may be on the wrong feet. He loves basketball. He loves sports. He's his father's son.

The score is tied. The ball is thrown to David. He shoots and scores. The crowd is on their feet. David pumps his fists. His fellow team mates are giving him high fives. He is a star. He will be smiling the rest of the day.

David is sixteen now and likes to do what typical sixteen year old boys like to do. He wrestles with his brother, plays board games, swims, rides horseback, plays with his cat, Louie, and plays golf.

"David, use the metal bat and not the plastic bat." Michael tells him as we are riding to the game. When it's David's turn to bat, he has the plastic bat. Michael goes to the dugout, picks up a metal bat and gives it to David. No words are spoken. David hits a ball to second base. David doesn't like to play the outfield and when he was younger, he sat down. Michael stood beside him in order to keep him standing. Michael is David's biggest cheerleader and best friend.

David has challenges, both mental and physical, but he loves life. Communicating is especially hard for him. The day before Mother's Day, Ric took both boys shopping for gifts for their mother. Ric bought a card where David could record a message. Though it took ten takes, David's voice was clear as he said "I love you Mom". Lori wept when she opened the card. David chose a pair of earrings for his mom and later in the day when Lori pointed to her ear to show him she was wearing them, he pointed to her other ear and said "Two!"

David's abilities are many and his challenges through the years have not been easy for him or his parents. Sleep disturbances are common with Down syndrome children. David was fourteen before he slept through the night. Because David's 21 Eustachian tubes are small, he has had countless ear surgeries because of chronic ear infections. Frequent sinus infections are another area that require attention. When he was one year old, he was diagnosed with hypothyroidism and takes a daily medication. This condition is present in ninety-five percent of children born with Down syndrome. From the time David was very young, he cried after eating. Ric and Lori took him to a specialist who diagnosed Celiac disease. Without a strict adherence to a gluten-free diet, nutrients are not absorbed.

When David was ten years old, he started losing his hair and alopecia universalis was diagnosed.

David is currently wearing braces. The Orthodontist isn't sure how successful the treatment will be because the roots of his teeth are very shallow. However, doing nothing to widen his palate and straighten his teeth would mean David would need jaw surgery later on.

Parenting a child with Down syndrome requires patience, stamina and an attitude of taking one day at a time. Lori gains strength by the love and support she has found in the community. She treasures the lessons she has learned in her journey as the parent of a disable child.

"David has affected people in so many ways; it's a blessing every day and I wouldn't have changed a thing."

Marie Sturge

Marie Sturge lives in Liverpool, New York with her husband. She is a graduate of Central City Business Institute. Marie enjoys spending time playing bridge, singing in her church choir and barbershop quartet, reading, gardening and playing golf. Marie enjoys writing and is currently working on a biographical novel. Marie volunteers at Cradle and Beyond, a non profit, selling new and slightly used clothing and house wares. She can be reached at Robertmarie78@verizon.net.

My Cat, Fish, and Grandma are in Heaven

Ever the optimist, my fifteen year old daughter views the world through different eyes. She could find the brightest of lights even in the darkest of situations. A glitch in her chromosomes may have caused her brain to be wired differently, but it also allowed her heart to be twice as big.

One of Elizabeth's favorite things to do is study the calendar. She memorizes everyone's birthday and will count down the days, or sometimes even the months, until it's time for them to blow out their candles.

When she announced out of the blue one day that I would be turning forty soon, I jokingly told her that this would be a special year and that she needed to throw me a surprise party.

"No" she said. "I can't do that."

"Why not?" I asked.

"Because you're going to be dead soon. Forty is close to one hundred, and when you turn one hundred you will die."

"I will?" I asked, wondering where she came up

with this logic.

"Yes, you are mom." she said matter-of-factly. "And then you will get to go up to your new home in heaven and see my cat, my fish, and my grandma!" She was getting very excited as she spoke.

"That will be nice to see them again" I said, shocked at her happiness.

"And when I'm one hundred, I'm going up to heaven to see them too." She gloated.

I had to smile at her outlook on life. To her, death wasn't a bad thing. Instead it is a wonderful opportunity to visit with those whom we are missing down here on Earth. Her mindset inspired me to look at things differently as well. So when the time comes for me to blow out my one hundred candles, I will close my eyes and wish for nothing more than to once again see my cat, fish, and grandma.

Amy Quonce

Amy Quonce is a multi-tasker extraordinaire who juggles working full time, driving her daughter to dance, and writing late at night when the rest of the house falls silent. Although there are no longer any cats or fish to enjoy, her daughter hopes to one day own a puppy that she can train to sit. They all still miss Grandma and Grandpa Scruton.

You can visit Amy's website at WindingRoadBook.Weebly.Com and email her at WindingRoadBook@aol.com.

Triumph Over Tragedy

At 20 weeks pregnant, my husband and I discovered that our unborn child would be born with a severe and rare spinal anomaly. The perinatologist offered us an option to escape the tragic possibilities that might lie ahead: termination of the pregnancy. We quickly answered, "No." Instead we prayed and researched and interviewed possible specialists. We hoped that our unborn child be born with a charming personality, friendly spirit, and strong will as we knew these qualities would help us sail through the difficult times ahead.

On December 16th, 2004 we welcomed little Chloe into the world. She was whisked away to NICU for *tests*. Chloe was born beautiful despite congenital spinal dislocation, caudal regression, tethered cord, fused ribs, decreased lung capacity, cloacal malformation, kidney reflux. *The road will be long* we thought *but worth it*.

The last 6 years for our family have been eventful and triumphant. Chloe has: spent over 200 days in various hospitals as an inpatient, 15 surgeries across 3 states, ambulance rides, intensive care unit stays…yet, these events travel with a pride and warmth that only a parent can describe. We are blanketed in the triumph.

Our little girl does not walk *yet*, but has charm I have not found in any other. Triumph for our family is profound; it exists in the choice we made over 6 years ago. The choice to hang onto hope and the life our hope blossomed into. Triumph is Chloe; delicate, armed with charm, strength, blue eyes, bright smile and… bright future.

Cari Joyce

Cari Joyce is a 2nd grade teacher who enjoys dabbling in writing short essays, newsletters, and articles. She writes for Move Along Inc. an organization that works to enhance athletic abilities for individuals with disabilities. Cari Joyce lives in Central New York with her husband, two children, and two dogs. This is her first published essay.

Lena's Smile

After sitting on the couch for an hour one evening, strapped to an airway clearance machine and having a nebulizer mask stuck to her face, Lena, my two year old daughter, gave me a hug and looked at me with those big eyes, as if she was thanking me for what I had been doing earlier that day. That afternoon I was hosting a bowling fundraiser to raise money for Cystic Fibrosis. This wasn't the first time my husband, family and friends were out there with me raising money and hosting fundraising events.

Lena was diagnosed with Cystic Fibrosis when she was only 13 days old. Cystic Fibrosis (CF) is a genetic cell disease where thick, sticky mucus builds up in the lungs and digestive system. There is no cure for Cystic Fibrosis and the median life expectancy is 37. As many times as I have said this, it doesn't get easier to accept.

I hate "treatment and vest time" and I love "treatment and vest time". It takes an hour every morning and an hour every evening, it's very time consuming. But during this time, I know that the medicine and the airway clearance machine are keeping Lena's lungs clear and healthy. Lena wears a vest that is connected to a machine that shakes her upper body in hopes of ridding her lungs of any mucus that could create an infection.

Lena is my little hero. She sits through her treatment and vest time with a smile on her face, not knowing that she has an ugly disease, despite how beautiful she is and she will have to do this for the rest of her life, as her disease will only get progressively worse. Every time Lena eats, she needs to take enzymes to help her digest and absorb food. She also takes a long list of other daily medications and dietary supplements. I don't know how she does it. I hate watching her being shook and given pills and inhaled medications. Why does such a sweet, little girl, have to go through all this? When it comes down to the blame game, it's my husbands fault and it's my fault. I hate our genes. But she did get big, beautiful hazel eyes.

When Lena was first diagnosed, John and I had a lot of adjusting to do. We were ready for a newborn, but not a newborn with Cystic Fibrosis. I'll admit that John and I were on a bumpy road for a bit, but here we are two years later, two expert Cystic Fibrosis parents, one little girl, one cat and a happy home. We were not going to let Cystic Fibrosis tear anything apart. In some ways, Cystic Fibrosis brought us closer. I think we both have been given such a blessing and know that even though Lena has CF, CF does not have Lena. We live with it, live around it, and live through it, but never will CF live with us! As much as I feel that CF takes control of her life, I'd like to hope we can ultimately take the wheel.

I've promised myself and Lena that I will never let Cystic Fibrosis win. I knew right from the start that I had to count on myself to get out there and do something about it, not to sit back and wait for the next CF parent to take control and find that cure. I dove right in to the Cystic Fibrosis Foundation. Speaking at a CF fundraiser, introducing a CF hero at a Cystic Fibrosis family event, attending a CF volunteer leadership conference and becoming the committee chair for the Oswego, New York Cystic Fibrosis Great Strides walk. I have done all these things because Lena was cursed with a disease that I hate, but because of this disease, there was a blessing in disguise.

Cystic Fibrosis is here to stay with Lena, but anyone who knows Lena, will tell you that there is just something about her. I'll tell you what that something is; it's how she smiles even though she has gone through more in her two years of life than anyone can imagine a little two year old could go through. It's how she smiles at the end of everyday and is thankful and blessed that the sun was shining or the rain was falling. It's how she smiles at you, when you have had the worst of days and somehow you forget all about how you wanted to scream and couldn't wait for the day to end. But that's Lena's smile, it's contagious.

Before John and I had Lena, our first pregnancy ended in miscarriage. When we first knew about the possibility of Lena having Cystic Fibrosis, I looked for a support group and couldn't find one. So I decided to start one. I was pointed in the direction to three other women who had experienced loss, health or disabilities with their children and grandchild. Soon enough the four of us women created a support group, PALS (pregnancy and loss support) of Oswego. A support group to help women and men just like us. I am very proud of our group. I took the miscarriage and Lena's disease and made it into something positive. I have watched many of the women in the group go on to have more children and learn to live and love and be blessed for anything that comes their way. I am included in that group.

Lena's CF has helped me learn to live life to it's fullest and love everything in it. To look at the world and embrace it. I've come very far in these past few years and I owe it all to my family, friends, Lena's doctors and staff, CF family and of course my smiling beauty, Lena. I have hope and faith that Lena will live to see that cure, because that smile of hers is something I just can't live without. So if you ever feel like you want to cry and can't stop asking "why", look at your child's smile. It's a blessing.

Lisa Elaine Williams

Lisa Williams lives in Oswego, NY with her husband, daughter and their cat, Bailey. She holds a Masters degree in Elementary Education and is currently a stay at home mom. Lisa enjoys spending her time going on day trips with her husband and daughter, spending time with her family and friends and bringing Lena to her dance classes. She also enjoys reading and hopes to write her own book about her experience with a miscarriage and her daughter's fight against Cystic Fibrosis. Lisa can often be found taking part in activities with the Cystic Fibrosis Foundation and a support group, PALS of Oswego, helping men and women who have experienced loss, disease or a disability with a child. If you would like to contact Lisa Williams you can email her at leaps4lena@yahoo.com.

Shatterproof

Today my husband left me with one job. That's not to say that my day wasn't already full; there was dishes, laundry, beds, vacuuming, my daughter's hair appointment, cooking, and of course there was the continuous care of my 12 year old autistic son. But thinking that I might be bored my husband suggested that I get that old set of glass French doors that have been in the backyard leaning against the house for the last 6 years, wrap them in an old tarp and break the glass out of them so that he can cut them up and take them to the dump. Sounds easy enough I think to myself and go merrily along on my routine filled day. Actually I forgot about them for several hours while I attempted to complete the day-to-day stuff. It wasn't until many hours later when my son and I finally got into the backyard for some free time that I recalled our other "job".

I look at the glass filled doors and remember all of the times that they have given me cardiac arrhythmias. .. like the time Adam was having a huge meltdown and hit his head on the wall and put a hole in the sheetrock and then went charging toward the glass to do a repeat but I caught him in time. Or the time when he threw his shoes directly at the glass because I was trying to get him to put them on without help or the time he shoved his twin sister and she surprised me by bouncing off instead of falling through. I can remember many conversations with my husband, my mother, my sister-in-laws, anyone that would listen how dangerous these windowed doors were and how I couldn't wait to get rid of them. Now I was having a hard time remembering them in place for they had been in my backyard for so long but I can't say I was missing them either! They are way too breakable, way too dangerous to have in my house. There is no place for something so fragile in my home; I need hard walls and sturdy boards to keep my family safe you know.

Well being a dutiful wife I wrapped those doors in an old tarp to contain the flying glass and got the trusty sledge hammer. Looking around to make sure that no one was too close; my son was happily playing in the pool, the dog was on the other side of the yard watching something (?), no silly squirrels in danger of being downed by shrapnel so. .I. ..swung. I swung that big ole sledge hammer over and down and hit the center of those glass doors and I heard. ..THUD. No, I didn't hear the tinkling of shattered glass or cascading shards. I heard a loud, dense THUD. I had to look; it just didn't sound right. There, wrapped so nicely in that old tarp were two shiny glass doors with nary a scratch!! I couldn't figure out HOW I had missed but that was the only explanation of course so I re-wrapped those darn doors in that old tarp and I took that big ole sledge hammer and I raised it above my shoulder and I took good aim and I let it drop right into the middle of those doors and I heard. .THUD! Okay, so I missed once. Perhaps I had only a glancing blow on the second carefully aimed blow but guess what happened on swing number three? You got it. ..THUD! Now, I'm all sweaty and I'm not very happy and I am very confused so it seemed like a great time to sit down and have a beer and watch my son play in the pool. He grins at me like "See, I told you it wouldn't break" and I give him a dirty look and tell him "Go jump in a pool!" which I guess is rather redundant but it felt good to say anyway. I finished that cold beer and decided that I would be the winner of this battle between middle aged woman and glass. The fourth hit was golden and all of the glass broke into long dull shards which is because it is safety glass my husband later tells me. Quite a lovely invention that safety glass. Sure wish I had known about it years before when I was having daily strokes with an out of control autistic toddler!

I realize now that those glass doors were symbolic for my son and his autism. Autism seems so clear sometimes. yet is not; it seems as if he is fragile yet he is very, very strong; he appears to be simple yet he is made up of some complex materials; nothing is as it appears. I would like to continue writing about my son, my family and our journey. Our next adventure starts in 9 days when we enter middle school. Am I worried? Maybe a little but I have learned that we are certainly NOT breakable!

Karen Delaney

Karen Delaney lives in Oswego, New York with her husband Dan and 14 year old twins, Adam and Erin. Karen started her working career as a registered nurse but since her son's autism diagnosis 12 years ago she has spent the majority of her days working with her son, advocating for him and others on the spectrum and trying to ensure a typical childhood for his sister. Karen enjoys being with her family, remodeling their home, gardening and working with technology. She is active in several organizations such as the Oswego County Autism Task Force and OPT IN (Oswego Parent/Teacher Inclusion Network) where Karen enjoys creating web site content, letter writing campaigns to the media and legislators as well as keeping the financial records. To contact Karen you can e-mail her at k.delaney@twcny.rr.com.

Feeding the Heart

"How's the little darling doing today?"
The nurse asks as she enters my room to
bring Elizabeth back to the nursery.

"She's still not nursing and as of yet no
wet diapers. Should I be concerned?"

"Now don't you worry, she'll eat when
she's good and ready. Tomorrow you'll be
heading home and once you're settled in
things will fall into place."

I smiled, trusting her judgment. *She did
have a traumatic entry into this world, and
that must have worn her body out. I'm sure
her appetite will perk up by tomorrow.*

My many attempts to feed Elizabeth the
rest of that day were spent with her trying to
nurse so hard that she ended up falling
asleep. By the time we were ready to be
discharged, I was still unsuccessful at
getting her to latch on for more than two
minutes, and she was still wearing the same

diaper that the NICU had put on her after the delivery.

The first twenty four hours at home was a concoction of high pitch screams and failed attempts to feed her. Nervous, I called the pediatrician to schedule an appointment for the following morning."I don't know what to do." I told the doctor. "She still won't nurse."

"Let's get a weight on her before I do the examination."Putting my newborn on the scales, I held my breath as I watched the doctor adjust the scale to her birth weight and then continued to slide the bar to the left. Down ¾ of a pound.

"I want you to start using bottles so that we can monitor exactly how much she is taking in. I'm going to schedule you for another appointment in two days to see if her weight has stabilized."

The doctor left the room and I bundle Elizabeth back up to leave. Putting the tabs back on her clean diaper I mentally noted how long she has had it on for.

Five days and counting.

Elizabeth's crying, while still constant, was getting weaker. Her tiny body was loosing it's strength. Whenever I put the nipple of the bottle in her mouth she would fight furiously to be able to grasp it, then fall asleep in defeat. The eight ounces that I had filled it with was still full by the next morning. Terrified, I rushed her down to the hospital's maternity ward to see the head nurse.

"Something is wrong. No matter how many times I try to feed her she isn't getting anything out. I slit the nipples open wider so that she wouldn't have to suck so hard but nothing is getting into her."

"How much did she weight at birth?" The nurse asked.

"7 pounds, 4 ounces."

"Put her in the scale."

My heart raced as it showed a mere 6 pounds 1 ounce. She has lost over a full pound in less than a week.

"We're going to have to try something different with her. I'm going to give you some tubing that we will tape to your finger. The other end will be attached to this bottle. I want you to try and have her suck on your finger, releasing the milk into her mouth."

"I'll try anything." I said. For three hours we sat in the hospital, working together to get drops of milk to fall onto my daughters' tiny tongue. Every attempt was failed.

"It's time to switch it up." The nurse

finally said. "She needs food and she needs it now."

I watched her walk down the hall and I picked up my daughter to hold her close. She looked so exhausted. Her dry lips curled down as she closed her droopy eyes and went to sleep. *Why can't she eat? I don't know how much longer she can go on like this.*

The nurse returned moments later with a small syringe in her hand. "We're going to bypass the mouth and drop the food directly down her throat. That way we know it's getting into her."

Rubbing my finger across her shriveled lips to open them, the nurse squirted the liquid into Elizabeth's mouth drop by drop. *It's working! Oh please let her be able to swallow it.* When the dropper was empty I breathed a little sigh of relief. We had managed to give her two ounces of formula…the most she has ever eaten in her entire life.

"Keep trying this at home until you see your pediatrician tomorrow."

"Thank you so much. You may have just saved her life."

On the way home there was a new sense of hope. Elizabeth was crying less and I contributed it to the fact that she had finally eaten. Washing her up before her doctors appointment the next morning I pulled some fresh clothes from her dresser. Next to that was the package of diapers that I had bought before she was born. Still sealed, they remained untouched as I once again put the dry diaper back on her that she had been wearing for a full week now. I pushed my growing fears aside and headed out the door for her next weight check.

"5 pounds, 8 ounces." The doctor announced. "Her skin is hanging off from her and she is completely dehydrated. I'm going to send you to a specialist for further testing."

The taste of salt falling onto my lips kept me from responding. All I could do was look at my baby and wonder how much longer I was going to have with her. Nobody knew what was wrong or how to help her. My daughter's cries for hunger were only matched by my tears for not knowing how to feed her. She was starving for nourishment and was withering away in front of my eyes.

"In the meantime I want you to try using the preemie nipples. They're designed to be easier to suck on than typical nipples. I also want you to wake her up every hour on the hour until you see the specialist. *Or she could die in her sleep* I thought.

Setting my alarm clock I took the new bottle and fed Elizabeth every fifty minutes. By the next morning she had managed to take in three whole ounces. While still very weak, I was pleased that the new nipples were helping. Getting her ready for a morning bath, I uncovered a small miracle.

Her diaper was wet!

All of our efforts had paid off. The crushing diagnosis given by the specialist that day was softened by the fact that she was going to live. A cleft palate was easily repaired, but her cognitive delays would have to be closely monitored. *As long as she's going to be okay, I can handle it.*

Over the next few years I became chief coordinator for the four therapists and fourteen specialists that would oversee her care. My world was now consumed by her needs, but the joy that she has brought to my life is priceless. Watching her learn to walk and talk despite the doctor's predictions inspired me to persue a career in Special Education. I found that there is no greater gift in life than having a special needs child touch your heart.

Amy Quonce

Elizabeth is currently in the 10th grade and working on her thirteenth year of studying dance. She enjoys listening to music, playing with her little cousins, and is counting down the days until her sweet 16th birthday party. When she graduates from school her dream is to become a veterinarian.

Collin

Having a child born with special needs has been at times trying. However, also a great and rewarding experience for my family and I. We've had opportunity to create life, nurture that life through good times and bad, while having an opportunity to meet some of the most wonderful people on Earth – caregivers, teachers and advocates. We as parents have grown having attended a support group for parents of children with special needs, which allowed us to develop lifelong friendships. Even though it took a lot of effort caring for our son Collin, our lives were limited more so than if we had a typical child. It was an experience that my family and I will never regret having. It has been the ride of our lives, but after all is said and done, it was a great ride.

My son Collin was our first of three children born. Initially, he seemed to have been born a happy and healthy baby boy.

Generally he would eat every few hours, woke maybe just a few times each evening, slept a lot, but he cried very little. In fact, Collins' crying decreased as time when on. Even so, after the first few months of his life, we as first time parents felt his crying less and less was cause for concern. When we brought this to the attention of Collins pediatrician, we were told "That we were just lucky parents, we had a content baby." However, deep down his father and I still felt that it was a cause for concern.

Another behavioral development we thought was concerning was that Collin would often fixate on objects that were round, or that went around like ceiling fans. Ceiling fans seemed to consume most of his attention. He even loved the tires on cars and would walk in circles.

At six months of age, I had received a frightening call from his grandmother.

"Baby Collin had a severe seizure, 911 emergency was called and they're transporting him to the hospital."

He was then first diagnosed with a seizure disorder, to what then started Collin on a lifelong, intense medication regiment. His seizures, in severity, were reduced and were less intense with the medications, but they would occur with greater frequency. With continued neurological care from Children's Hospital in Buffalo NY, Collin's seizures became less frequent.

While there, we were approached to allow Collin to participate in a trial pharmaceutical seizure study. The study required a considerable commitment focused on seizure medication development. Collin would receive constant monitoring, both short and long hospital stays, difficult bouts of pain, and struggles of increased and decreased seizure activity. Reluctantly, my husband and I agreed to allow Collin to participate in said trial study, not only to hopefully help Collin, but maybe many more children as well. You'd figure most children during all of these seizures, medications, shots, IV's and doctors appointments would be unhappy, fed up, dejected... not our beautiful son, Collin. He always seemed to be his happy content self. In fact, he would now often go months without crying.

We again brought our concerns to the attention of his pediatrician; as we knew something was wrong and demanded the doctors to address it. He was now beginning to fall behind in his cogitative development as well. Doctors ordered an Early Intervention referral and he was deemed eligible for services. The early intervention support services started right away, he was given Speech, OT, PT and Special Education services.

All the services were excellent for Collin, but often at times overwhelmingly hard on him, on top of the schedule of two working parents. About six months after the Early Intervention began, concerns were noted regarding his behaviors and apparent cognitive developmental delay. It was suggested that we should get him evaluated at a Pediatric Developmental Center.

We went through many highs and lows in completing the evaluation, travel back and fourth, cancellations, and rescheduled appointments, all along with Collin's seizure activity. At the conclusion of the evaluation, Collin was diagnosed with Autism. In retrospect we should have been shocked but deep down we had already suspected this diagnosis.

Over the years, Collin took many different medications. But there was one in particular that did wonders for his seizure control, Topomax. To us it seemed like the miracle drug, as it worked very well controlling his seizures and it was at this time that Collin had begun to flourish. He blossomed to speak several words. He could count, start to say some of his ABC's, and could even express his wants and needs.

Then there were times of regression. Once over February break on his Kindergarten year of school, all of Collin's speech disappeared. All he could do was grunt. The doctor's quickly changed his medication regimen. Unfortunately, over the years he was only able gain back 8-10 words of his vocabulary. Even though Collin didn't use many words, he was able to communicate with others.

Collin had a look in his eyes that would melt your heart. He was a very personable and friendly young man. He loved other people, especially women. When in the store, if you stopped to look at something he would simply walk up to the next woman he found, take her hand and start walking with her. When we went camping, he would often run off to other people's campsites and try to bring back any ladies that were there. They all fell in love with him right away. Over the last few years, Collin's personality had just gotten so loveable. He loved to cuddle and smile with you. He loved to be tickled and he loved to say "Hi" back and forth with you. He loved the attention and interaction.

Children have a unique sense of when someone or something is amiss. Almost like knowing a storm is coming before it gets here feeling. My children, Austin and Shiann, proved this openly to my husband and me. Being that they are younger than Collin, they still had the ability to be very aware and they knew their brother was different. They knew they had a special responsibility towards their brother, and they did this with great pride. For example, Austin felt in his own heart how he wanted to be the one to educate his fellow students in school. He did this by "showing them", on his own terms, how to feel comfortable around Collin and not to be afraid of his expressions, or behaviors. Both of the children, I know, will always remember Collin and hold their relationship they had with him, for the rest of their lives.

We lost our beautiful Collin early one morning, so quickly that we could not even say good-bye. Maybe he planned it this way, as I felt he was so much in touch with things and situations that I cannot even explain. Collin knew it was time to leave this beautiful plane and travel to a new one. He heard someone call his name. My son, even though wrought with seizures and autistic, was truly a deep thinker. He gave us joy, he gave us love, and he gave us wonderful memories.

My life is not what it was, nor will it ever be, but I know that sweet boy, who meant so much to us and also to everyone who knew him, would want us to get as much excitement as he did from the simple, beautiful things in life, like things that are round or go around.

Marie Smith

Marie Smith lives in a small rural town called Parish New York. She is married to a wonderful man named Rob and has three beautiful children. Her older son is named Austin. He is an ambitious little boy who is always working towards some kind of goal. Her daughter is named Shiann who is constantly trying to keep up with her older brother. Marie is also the mother of a very beautiful angel in heaven named Collin. The family also has two dogs.

Marie has many hobbies, but most of them include her children as they are the most important part of her life. Marie enjoys camping with her family, going for bike rides with her family, and taking the kids to parks and bounce houses. She also enjoys reading.

Marie has an Associates Degree in community social services earned from Cazenovia College as well as a Bachelor's Degree in human services from the University of Phoenix online. Marie has learned a lot from her education but she will tell you that it does not compare to what she has learned through experiences relating to having children, especially one with special needs.

Marie has had many employment opportunities throughout her life. In high school, she did a lot of babysitting and worked at a basket factory learning how to make the wood that baskets are made of as well as how to make the baskets. In college, she worked at a dinning hall, at a day care, and as a monster at a haunted hay ride. After college, she worked at a group home with people that had Developmental Disabilities, at the New York State Fair grandstand, and a family owned restaurant. Currently, she is a Medicaid Service Coordinator for Arise in Oswego County. Marie will tell you that she has learned something valuable from each and every one of these opportunities.

Marie has had many other helpful contacts throughout the last nine years since she has become the mother of a child with a disability. She has worked closely with Arise through service coordination. She has also been an active participant of Parents of Special Children where both she and her husband attended an Autism connection support group for parents of children with Autism. She will tell you that it is a very supportive group of friends. She will also tell you that she has had many other contacts related to her son Collin with respite programs and training opportunities throughout the years.

This has been Marie's first attempt at any formal writing. It has been interesting and difficult as the wound of loosing her oldest child at the age of nine is still very fresh. Collin was easy to write about though because he was a very interesting child and very important to his mother.

Stella's View

Mommy, I can see you,
standing in the rain
Mommy, I can feel you,
and I know your pain
We should be together, holding one another
Telling silly stories, underneath the covers
Mommy…I can see you…
waiting for the train.
Daddy, I can see you,
lost and feeling low
Daddy, I can feel you,
you don't know where to go
We should be together, playing peek-a-boo
Making silly faces, and saying 'I love you'

Daddy... I can see you...

wandering to and fro.

Jesus, I can see you,

your smile warms my face

Jesus, I can feel you,

you fill me with your grace

I'm glad that we're together, living in the
sky

Yet sorry that my death caused both of them
to cry

Jesus...I can see you...

and feel your warm embrace.

Debbie Hough

*Debbie Hough is the mother of three grown
children and the grandmother of six – five of which
she can play with and one who plays with angels.
Debbie spends her free time quilting, reading,
volunteering, and writing her weekly column in the
local paper. You can get to know her better at*

www.commakazes.com , a web site for her writers group.

Debbie loves children and believes they are God's greatest invention.

A Grandson Like No Other

Tyler is my grandson. He's 16. He talks --
a lot, as a result of having brain damage as a
child due to hydrocephalus caused by an
arachnoid cyst in his brain, diagnosed at age
13 months, resulting in two brain surgeries.
The family was devastated, but we saw him
through it, and Tyler has become an
interesting contradiction of what any of us
could have imagined. He's funny, smart,
annoying, analytical, stubborn, able to laugh
at himself, inquisitive, exasperating (**really**
exasperating), compassionate, intrusive,
positive, and knows everything about
everything, just ask him!

He loves the computer, and we spend
time together playing our favorite online
game, Blob Wars. I don't remember
winning, maybe once, and Tyler takes great
pleasure in that, laughing at me every time
he wins, I don't think it's that funny. We also
took a virtual tour through all the historic

sites of San Francisco via a hidden objects game. We persevered through 64 levels, gaining a pretty good knowledge of the city of San Francisco as a bonus.

My mother lived with my husband and me for nearly two years, and passed away this past May at 90 years old. She was GeGe to Tyler, and he loved spending time with her too. He'd lie on her bed while she watched TV, drawing or playing his DS or computer games. I'd hear them talking and laughing. She would tell him stories about how things were when she was growing up, and all the things they didn't have that we now take for granted. He'd help her with different things, wait on her, bringing her snacks and drinks, or making her lunch and taking it to her in her room, sitting with her as she ate. She would always become frustrated with her TV remote control, push a wrong button, become impatient, and just start pushing all the buttons or banging it on the arm of her chair, saying the battery was probably dead, when in fact she'd hit a button requiring the push of a button to reset. Tyler would very patiently explain to her once again, how it worked and then reset it. Sometimes I'd hear him discussing with her why it was important to wear her oxygen and keep her feet elevated. GeGe was very impressed with Tyler, especially his excellent grammar and how well he could spell, and thought he was "a very intelligent young man, very well spoken."

Tyler has a friend who is in classes with him at school, who broke her ankle. Tyler was right there by her side, helping her along throughout the day, and is very protective of her, and she, in turn, helps him remember things. They compliment each other quite well. He seems to have a special place in his big heart for kids who are bullied, and in fact has lunch many days with a boy who bullied him, once hitting Tyler in the face. Tyler sits with him because no one else does, and he doesn't want him to eat lunch alone. It seems no matter what life throws at Tyler, he manages to maintain a confident, positive, happy attitude, a very unique young man.

BJ Solazzo

My Silly Girl

I have several grandsons, but only one granddaughter, Elizabeth Megan. Such a beautiful name for such a beautiful girl. She is a happy child who recently celebrated her 15th birthday. Who would have known she would come this far?

While still in her mother's womb, the doctors warned us of complications and although they were right, she was born far better off than we were led to believe. And with Elizabeth's birth, her journey began.

Over the years, there have been so many doctor visits and hospitalizations that I lost track. I don't know how her mother kept it all straight. To me, it was mind-boggling. It takes a special parent to deal with a special need child. I am not sure if I could have handled it. I would like to think I could have dealt with all the complications if I had to, but honestly, I don't know. It is hard to put yourself in someone else's shoes. I give my daughter Amy a lot of credit. She had patience with her daughter that surprised me and continues to amaze me.

Elizabeth was a beautiful child right from birth. Dark hair, dark eyes, but she could not smile. That tiny little face was always the same, expressionless. Plus, there was the problem with the consistent vomiting and the fact that she nearly died more than once. I really thought she would. Both my mom and I were worried. She endured a lot, and yet she survived, due to not only professional medical care, but to the continuous care of her mother. Her diligent watch over her daughter kept Elizabeth from tumbling off this edge of life until she was strong enough to flourish on her own.

Elizabeth, or Lizzy as I found myself calling her, wasn't one of those babies that cried often, but she did when her mother would leave her for what Lizzy must have thought as 'too long.' The first few hours she was happy as a lark as we took turns entertaining her. But after that, she would toddle off to the window staring outside and cry. Nothing would distract her. Her Aunt Katrina would take her in her bedroom to play music, but the crying continued. Her Uncle Chad would bundle her into his arms and try soothing her with rocking motion as he wandered around the house cradling her but the crying continued. Not even when I would pick her up, dancing around the living room with her in my arms, would that pacify her. She just wanted her mamma. The crying continued until her mamma walked through the door, to our relief. This happened so many times that I finally told Amy that I would only watch Liz for two hours intervals; it wasn't fair to make that child suffer. I think Liz's emotional state was like grieving. She felt the loss of her mother. Since Elizabeth could not communicate her wishes, we were always guessing. It was a very difficult time.

As a toddler and unable to speak, Lizzy would become frustrated with the lack of communication, she would end up throwing herself on the floor crying hectically. I told my daughter that her tantrums were due to the fact that she was trying hard to let us know something. I felt so bad for that poor little baby. She didn't know what else to do to get us to understand and we were doing everything we knew to understand. We were at a dead spot. We needed help and knew it.

At this point, the doctors thought teaching her sign language would help. And, it sure did the trick. Her little fingers flew. For the first time, Lizzy was able to tell us she wanted a glass of milk, or that she was enjoying watching the dancers on stage at a concert, or if she wanted us to read her a book. The tantrums stopped altogether. I believe this was a huge breakthrough. Now, she was 'one of us.' Communication is the link between humans. Eventually, the doctor performed several surgeries on her. First they repaired the cleft palette and then later they placed a pharyngeal flap in her mouth, enabling her to finally learn how to speak at age six.

Another problem that we had to face with Liz is that she was afraid of things…like play-doh and soap. She would scream in fear if anything of that texture was near her. With the help from Early Intervention, she was able to overcome these fears, as well as others. Because of the help she received, many of the problems that plagued her during her pre-school years slowly disappeared.

I know my daughter was heartbroken for years when she would listen to her little nephew David, who was three months younger than Elizabeth, giggle and smile with excitement, as most babies do.

However, Liz had never giggled or smiled during her babyhood. Not once. The years passed.

Then the day came when Lizzy smiled for the first time. I can't explain the joy we all experienced. It took several surgeries, but the doctors were able to give Lizzy a smile! The medical staff may not have an exact name for her condition but they fixed what they could. That little girl is blessed to live in a time where miracles are performed.

As the years and struggles continued to go behind us, newer brighter days came. Lizzy was growing up. Even today she continues to play with her various decks of cards stacked in columns that she has collected over the years, or the hundreds of books that she piles onto her bed as her nightly ritual, and yet she loves to dance and sing just like any teenage girl.

Lizzy started dance lessons when she was still no more than a toddler. The first few years of recitals, she just stood on stage for the most part. Many do at that age. But with the passing of time, you could see her blossom right up there on that stage. She knew the steps to each dance whether it was ballet, tap, jazz, hip hop or lyrical. She kept up with the group dancers. Music and dance is what she thrives on. It has opened a whole new world for her. This is Lizzy's world. It has given her a focus, something that she can excel at, something that she totally enjoys and connects to.

Elizabeth Megan loves everybody and everything. There is not a negative bone in her body. She lives in a world of happiness and showers it on to others. She is easy going, talkative, friendly and she makes me smile.

To use one of Elizabeth's favorite terms, "I love my girl. You're my silly girl."

Connie Scruton (A.K.A. Nana)

Connie Scruton is a freelance writer and a noted columnist of Minglings, featured in the Palladium Times. She is credited with articles written for the United Way and Red Cross. She wrote her first story at the age of 11; a comedy that won her praise from her teacher with an A+, and classmates as they rolled with laughter. Currently, she is working on a true-life novel of an event dealing with the supernatural.

Life as a Sibling to a Special Needs Child

Michael Bryon Sill was born twenty three months after his brother, David Francis, who was born with Down Syndrome. By the time Michael was two years old, he was already looking out for his brother.

David was introduced to American Sign Language when he was a little tyke and by the time Michael was six months old, Michael had picked up the sign for "more". He actually signed before he spoke his first words! I found that absolutely amazing.

One winter day when Lori had taken David to pre-school, she stopped over with Michael who was two at the time. Grandpa came in the door shortly after and Michael said "Papa, shoes, door". Grandpa looked at Lori and asked what he was trying to say. Lori replied, "He wants you to shut the door and take off your shoes!" Even though

David was not with them, he knew to keep cellar doors closed so David would not fall down the stairs.

There is such love between these brothers. I have a picture of Lori holding David on her hospital bed while he looks into Mikey's little bed and he is moving the blanket to get a better look. Another picture shows David on his knees trying to kiss Michael as he sits in his baby seat.

Ric and Lori wanted Michael to be exposed to special needs children other than his brother so when the time came for Mike to attend preschool, they chose Main Street School in North Syracuse where David had attended.

David was six and Mike was four when David was diagnosed with Celiac Disease. Even at that age, Michael kept a close eye on what David could and couldn't eat. When they were outdoors playing, Michael held David's hand to cross the street or prevent him from chasing a ball into the street.

When Mike was seven, he decided to write a book about his life with David complete with pictures. He titled the book, "My Brother David". The dedication is to "My big, small brother"! In the first chapter, the picture shows baby David, complete with his oxygen tubing sitting with stuffed animals twice his size. Chapter 3 tells about David taking part in Special Olympics when he was eight years old. The picture shows him wearing a silver medal he had won. Another chapter shows him strumming a guitar. Michael writes "Whenever we get in the car, David says, "SING!" Chapter 5 shows our entire family at the Down Syndrome Buddy Walk. All of us are in white tee shirts with David's picture on the front. Future chapters show him playing soccer, basketball and baseball. The final chapter shows a picture of the two of them in a chair with David kissing his baby brother. The words on the page are "My brother and I are BEST friends! I love my brother VERY much".

When David was learning addition and vocabulary, Michael used flash cards to help him. He gave him a "prize" if he did a good job. Michael assists on the Special Olympics sports teams. If we play a game when they come to visit, Mike always says, "Let's play a game David can play."

Being the sibling of a child with special needs is not all fun and games. From the time Michael was young, he tagged along to the many doctor appointments, sporting events and Down Syndrome Association dances and picnics. Sometimes Michael is embarrassed because David can be loud. When he is over stimulated, he makes strange sounds. Because David has Alopecia, he is bald and looks different. Most of the time, Michael handles these situations well, but even so, it can be difficult. Michael's friends love David and when they see him, they give him a high five or the girls give him a hug. If Mike and his friends are playing a sport or swimming, David is part of the group. However, there are times when David isn't included. David has learned to entertain himself well and takes it in stride.

The special needs child is the focus of attention in the family. This too, can be hard on a sibling. From the time David was born, he has had many medical issues that entail numerous doctor visits and a need for special attention at home. Sometimes the sibling feels he needs more attention than what he is receiving. Both Ric and Lori make a special effort to spend one on one time with Michael.

Expectations are different for each of the boys when it comes to chores and sometimes Michael thinks David is getting off too easy. There are some tasks David simply can't do.

It always amazes me when I take care of them and can't understand what David is trying to say or can't understand the sign he is using. Michael knows. He is the translator. If I am unsure if David can eat a certain food, Michael knows what he can and can't have.

David loves mascots. Whenever they go to a sporting event where there is a mascot, David gets their autograph and has his picture taken with the mascot. Recently, they were at a Boston Red Sox game and when the mascot came off the field, he went straight to the locker room and didn't sign autographs. Later in the game, Mike said to David, "Give me your baseball and I'll see if I can get Wallie's autograph." He didn't get the autograph but instead autographed it himself with Wallie's signature. David was happy which meant everyone was happy. David wants to be a mascot when he grows up!

Michael is very proud of David. He is extremely kind to his brother and they have a close bond. I know Michael will always look out for his brother. They are both Freshman in high school at the Liverpool

Annex. David is 16 and Mike is 14. David will stay in school until he is 21.

Marie Sturge

Marie Sturge is the mother of two, step mother of six and grandmother of fourteen. After seeing an article in the local paper advertising writing classes being offered at the local library, she signed up and started writing essays and short stories. Reading is a huge source of enjoyment for her as is playing bridge, singing in her church choir and barbershop quartet, playing golf and gardening. She lives two blocks from her son's family and enjoys watching her grandsons participate in their many activities. If you would like to contact her, she can be reached at: Robertmarie78@verizon.net.

Star's are Born in Performing Arts

As teachers for the performing arts at our local YMCA, my sister Kaylee and I have gotten the opportunity to work closely with people who have been diagnosed with various disabilities. Through spending time with them each week, we have not only shaped their lives, but they have influenced ours as well.

After announcing to our group that they would be putting on a small production from the movie Grease at the annual holiday party, the room lit up. We all turned to each other and smiled for we knew we we're in the right place; we felt happiness and joy within our hearts. It made us feel good to know that they were happy and already having a good time. Twice a week we got together as a group to rehearse, play games, and socialize with one another. I think we look forward to these days more than the kids did. It was a time when we knew that everyone was accepted for who they were, and friendship reigned over anything else.

As we started working on learning the song and dance moves to coordinate with the song lyrics, we were amazed on how much talent that emerged from them. Some seemed to be more into acting than others, and some more into music than acting, and some seemed to be interested in both. The talent they possessed was diverse as the individuals themselves, but together they drove the passion to keep one another on task.

Each activity we did with the class was set up to teach them something, anywhere from working better with people in a group, to giving them more confidence in completing things, to just having fun. They are very quick learners, and not everybody realizes just how smart people with a disability really are. They can do a lot more than what others give them credit for. If you give them the direction and guidance they need, they are capable of doing just about anything. And if you offer them the respect that they deserve, you will receive all the love in the world from them in return. They will also teach you some of life's greatest lessons.

Our students really enjoyed taking part in class. They loved the singing, dancing, and acting. They were able to have the chance to show their talent, gain confidence within their selves and their abilities. Since we have started our group, within our class has emerged a song writer, a voice impersonator, a comedian, some actors, actresses, and dancers. One boy in our group has even been inspired to write his own songs and share them with us. They are all so talented and we are proud of each one of them. They had the opportunity to learn and be guided by us and to take away more knowledge on performing arts as well as taking this knowledge and applying it to their lives.

The love that each one of our students possesses never ceases to amaze us. Just as we supported them in their ventures, they did the same for us. When we announced that we had upcoming auditions in the performing arts, they ran right up to us and gave us hugs. It warmed our hearts knowing that they cared for us just as much as we care for them. We are each other's cheerleaders in life. We work together, learn from each other, and inspire one another.

Kaylee and I are honored to be working

as a performing arts teacher for the Oswego YMCA respite. I am glad to have had the two of them with me to experience this wonderful journey. This is our first experience working with differently-abled individuals, and we have enjoyed being able to see how much strength and passion they have within.

This has been a very rewarding opportunity for all three of us, as we have had the chance to meet and work with an amazing and very artistic group of people. I can't wait to show everyone just how talented they are and how hard they have worked at the holiday party in December where everyone will be able to see their performance of the song " Your the one that I want", from the movie Grease. It will be their night to shine. Stars are born in performing arts, and we know that each and every one in our group will rise to the challenge.

This program has changed our lives and to know that it changed theirs is very rewarding on its own. It is going to be sad when it's over with, but I'm sure we will be keeping in touch with everyone and see them again someday. When we do I know that whatever they are doing with their lives it will have meaning to them and they will be very successful at it.

I am looking forward to working more with people who have a disability. We are proud to be among the first three people to start a performing arts program for respite at the YMCA, and we hope to see it expand world wide. I hope our story has inspired many to look beyond the label and see the inner strength that lies inside. Don't look at them as different, because they aren't. They are all the same, very loving, smart, kind, and caring individuals, and if given the a little time and patience you will be amazed at what they can do. Remember, when God makes us different from others, it's his way of letting everyone know we are very special.

Kevina and Kaylee Schleicher

Kevina Schleicher works as a performing arts teacher for the Oswego YMCA. This is her first experience working with people of various disabilities and has enjoyed being able to see how much strength and passion they possess. Kevina is 19 years old and she enjoys acting, singing, modeling, running, helping others, cooking, drawing, reading, learning, traveling, and photography. She hopes to one day move to Hollywood to pursue an acting career. You can reach Kevina at kevinaschleicher@gmail.com.

Kaylee Schleicher works as an assistant for the Oswego YMCA Performing Arts Club. She is 15 years old and she enjoys acting, singing, cooking, baking, helping people, cutting hair, and drawing. Someday she hopes to be a hairdresser or a chef. You can reach Kaylee at: Kayleee_S@yahoo.com.

A Dog's Tale

My name is Velcro. I am special. What makes me special is my relationship with my human partner. You see, I'm a dog. But I'm not just any dog – I'm a service dog. I was born, raised and trained to be partnered with a person with a disability. In July of 2003 I was paired up with Sarah, a 16-year-old girl who has been paralyzed from mid-back down since birth. It was quite a journey just to get with Sarah.

I was born on November 6, 2000. When I was old enough to leave my mom I went to a puppy trainer. I learned a lot of good things there that would help me become a service dog. I started to get used to being around people. To be honest, I learned a few bad things, too, like learning to drink coffee out of a cup. I lived there 'til I was a year old.

From there my training got serious. Quite a few dogs don't make it. It's not that they're not smart enough or unfriendly. Most fail because they're too friendly – they bark or try to run to strangers they'd like to

meet. Fortunately, I made the cut. I was
ready to meet my partner. The worst part of
it for me – besides leaving my puppy raiser
and other people I loved – was having to
live in a kennel at Canine Working
Companions. I hate kennels!

The best day of my life came in July
2003. That's when I met Sarah. She stayed
there from Monday to Friday for two weeks
so that we could work together and become
a team. I can turn light switches on and off,
pick up things she drops, open the
refrigerator and pull her wheelchair. Most
importantly, I am her companion. One of the
worst days of my life was the first Friday
when Sarah went home for the weekend. I
had to go back to my kennel (during the
week I slept in her room). It was so great on
Monday when she came back. We practiced
more and I got to go out with her in public. I
was so happy when, at the end of our second
week, I went home with her. I never want to
see a kennel again!

That September I started school with
Sarah. She and her folks were kinda nervous
about that. They weren't sure how teachers
and other students would react. In a way,
they had reason to worry (I'll get to that
later). I was very popular. Students and

teachers alike had never seen a dog attending high school. I had to lie down under or next to Sarah's desk. But I was never bored – it was great being able to spend the day with her when everybody else's dog had to stay home.

One of the fun things I got to do was be in marching band. Sarah played bells and synthesizer in the "pit" (percussion and other instruments that didn't march, but played on the sideline). It woulda been hard for her to march in a wheelchair even if I helped. Some of the band moms made a band uniform for me. All the kids wanted to be on my bus when the band traveled to shows.

Earlier I mentioned that my family had a reason to be worried about me in high school. That reason is that I got REALLY spoiled. Some of Sarah's teachers liked to give me treats. Did I mention that I love to eat? One day when we were changing classes, instead of pulling her nicely down the hall I took off running to the teachers' lounge. They had food there. I was so fast that Sarah had to let go. She was afraid her chair would tip over or crash into something or someone. As a result, we had to do some remedial work when it came time for me to be recertified.

We had another bad experience (I still don't think I misbehaved). Sarah played in the school orchestra. I got to be with her during rehearsal and even during a concert. At one concert I was having so much fun I decided to join in. I jumped up – knocking over Sarah's music stand – and started singing along. The audience loved me! Unfortunately, Sarah and the orchestra director weren't pleased. I could still go to concerts after that, but I had to stay in the audience with Sarah's parents.

February 2004 was when I got my best dog friend. Sarah's parents bought a Golden Retriever puppy. Her name is Emma. I got to go along to get her, so that we could meet before she moved in. Over the years, Emma and I have had some good times. We both like going out for ice cream. She might have been a little jealous because when Sarah went out to a restaurant or shopping I got to go and she had to stay home.

In our senior year the school yearbook devoted a half a page to me – seems being the school's first canine was a big deal. I hafta admit, though, that my high school years were fun. And it's kinda cool being a 4-year-old high school graduate.

Sarah attended Buffalo State College and I went with her. The only accessible rooms were in the suites for upper classmen. As a freshman, Sarah didn't have many friends in her dorm. She had me, though, and I like to think that made a big difference. Having a dog is also a good way to meet people.

Sarah graduated from college in 2009 and got a job in her field. Through it all I was there to help any way I could. One of our happiest days was in May, 2010. That's when Sarah and her boyfriend, Ben, got married. I got to be in the wedding. Now I live with them in a house they bought last spring. We have a big yard which I really enjoy.

If I could tell people one thing about service dogs, it would be to realize that when their vest is on be respectful of the fact that they are working. No one wants to be distracted when they are on the job. I love people and the attention they give me. But if it interferes with my ability to help Sarah it's not good.

I love my job because I love Sarah. When someday she gets another dog I hope it realizes how lucky it is.

Velcro Townsend & Steve Ingerson

Steve Ingerson is a United Methodist minister. He lives in Minetto, New York with his wife of 36 years, Sabine. Steve has been on disability leave since 2008 for fibromyalgia. His interests include photography, writing, art, music and reading.

In January 1987 Sabine and Steve's third child, Sarah, was born in the 25th week of pregnancy at 1 pound 14 ounces. It was a long haul for their family. Sarah is paralyzed from mid-back and has asthma. She spent her first 6 months in the NICU and required 24 hour nursing coverage when she came home as she was on a ventilator. During her childhood she was hospitalized often and required several surgeries. Sabine and Steve tried to provide Sarah and their other children, Sonya and Eric, as "normal" a home as possible.

What I Learned

What I have learned from having a Special Needs Child is to never accept inequality for your child. This is true for any mother, but even more so with a Special Needs child.

When you strive for this, you do get more. I have met some wonderful people along the way, especially when they let me try to run with the Oswego Middle School modified track team because my son needed a one to one at the time.

It became apparent that I could not compete with the boys, but Derek could follow them. The coaches decided to have me become like a crossing guard so the boys could be protected when running onto the other road that led to the water treatment plant.

Later, my son received the MVP medal in a local school track meet with Pulaski, Fulton and Oswego.

Kim Grindle

Age is Only a Number

Once upon a time there was a little girl who enjoyed spending afternoons with her Uncle. Four times a week she skipped down the sidewalk with her brown and blonde ringlets bouncing from left to right in beat with her singing. While her parents enjoyed a couple hours exercising at the YMCA, she played with her uncle. Of course her parents thought he was "watching" her but…

As we walked a few miles on the treadmill, worked out on the machines, or took a class, the uncle standing nearly seven foot and his precious five-year-old niece were up to Mischief, with a capital M. Unaware to this little girl's parents, once they made their way across the parking lot to enjoy each other's company while getting in shape…the children were at play.

This particular evening her parents decided to skip their showers so they could treat their sweet daughter to McDonald's. While Dad put the bags in the car, Mom made her way next store to ring the buzzer. Once inside the corridor they could hear a familiar giggle echoing from the other end of the hall. "Oh no, it sounds like they are having fun but I hope they haven't disturbed your brother's neighbors." As her father rounded the corner he spied a tiny flash of energy run into the apartment. Her parents followed the cookie trail of laughter only to find water everywhere!

There was water on the walls, the floor, and even sprinkled as evidence on their daughter's clothes. "What happened? Where did all the water come from?" Neither the uncle nor the child answer but look in the other direction. The parents look at each other and smile. Overlooking the obvious her parents decide to let it go because they know she is in good hands and well taken care of. "It's a onetime thing, right?" She laughed all the way to McDonald's. I wonder what happened tonight.

Less than a week later her parents arrive at the apartment to a similar scene but this time there is water in the hall. "What is going on? Now there is water on the walls in the hall." Skeptical and concerned the little girl's parents sneak into the apartment to see their sweet dumpling jumping up and down on her uncle's bed squirting a water gun towards the kitchen until...

Until, she looks up and sees her parents staring in disbelief at her. There is an instant freeze frame that last only a moment. Then her dear Uncle jumps from the kitchen towards the bed and super soaks her. She doesn't shoot back but instead points towards the hall. He peeks his head around the corner, smiles, and shoots! Yes he did! He super soaked us too. The innocence of our daughter polluted as she watches her uncle break the rules right in front of us. In less than a minute all four of us are laughing and enjoying the moment.

After some convincing the water guns are emptied and put away. We remind the dear uncle the importance of boundaries for our daughter. He responds with, "I know she told me but I told her this is my house not yours." And then he smiles at us with the innocence of our five year old. In spite of being thirty-eight years older than his niece he exuberates joy and energy into all he does. The following week I would like to tell you they refrained from having a water gun fight but I can't.

The following week they snuck in a walk to the nearest grocery store to purchase more water guns. "Why did you need more water guns?" we asked when we returned to a water-soaked apartment once again. Their response was both in unison and priceless – "But everyone else wanted to play."

"Everyone?" We are afraid to ask yet for the safety of our daughter and for the sake of her dear uncle's apartment lease we ask the question. "Who is everyone?" My daughter smiled at us and started her dissertation – "You raised me to make friends and share. The people in the hall were watching us play and laughing so I invited them to play. They didn't have any water guns so we walked to the Big M and we bought them for everyone. Everyone played Mom and Dad. It was so much fun." I could only shake my head. My husband stares down his brother and our daughter; well she grabs her uncle's hand and leads him into the kitchen.

With her little finger she beckons him to lean down but instead he scoops her up into his arms, "What is it little one?" She kissed his cheek and then whispers in his ear – "We need to hide the water guns so we can play again next time." He nods and the guns are hidden. As much as we tried, the water gun wars continued with laughter, memories, and a bond never to be broken between a five-year-old and her Big Bird of an uncle.

I learned a valuable lesson through this experience. First – when I trust our daughter to her uncle, be prepared for anything yet knowing she is always safe and the center of his attention. Second, it doesn't matter how old a person is that determines the amount of responsibility or fun they will have but instead it is the age of their heart and mind. We are blessed with a daughter who sees the fun and good in everyone and with an uncle who enjoys being a kid. I pray you take time to play today and see the world through the eyes of a child – regardless of their age.

Lisa Buske

In addition to teaching, writing, and speaking – Lisa M. Buske enjoys spending time with her family and friends. From time spent at the nursing home as a child to working with an array of special needs children, she truly enjoys the diversity and youth warmly wrapped within a person.

Through The Eyes of a Child

My sister and I are exactly 12 months and 4 days apart. We were both pregnant at the same time – our due dates were 5 months apart. But she went late, and 11 weeks later I found myself having an emergency C-section.

She knew in advance that her daughter, Elizabeth, was going to be born with problems. My baby, David, came into this world early, so I had no idea what was ahead of me. Luckily, he ended up with no problems at all. "Liz", as I call her, had a lot.

When they got to be toddlers, I would get excited as my son would reach certain milestones, or learned something new. But it was hard to share that excitement, because her baby wasn't up to the same level. It was hard not to compare, because they were so close in age. I always felt a little guilty showing him off.

David knew Liz since he was born, so I think he accepted her for who she was. He would try to play with her when they came over. He would always go get a toy and ask if she wanted to play. She couldn't talk, but she would shake her head. He would get another, and again, she would shake her head. She was happy to find a Memory game. Eventually David would give up trying to find something for them to play, and ask if she wanted him to play the game with her. Of course she didn't. She was happy just stacking the cards over and over.

When they started school, theirs was the only one in the district that accepted special needs kids. I wondered if David would go to school and pretend he didn't know Liz, but he didn't. He saw other "special" children, each in their own way, and would come home to tell me about them. I remember watching their Kindergarten Christmas play. Each kid in their own cute costume. You could tell the "special" ones – they would be the ones that the teachers had to hold the antlers on their heads because they didn't like hats, or the ones who had to cover their ears when the singing got too loud. But it didn't matter to the audience, or even to the kids themselves. Everyone did great, and the whole audience loved it.

Over the years, I heard many stories about these kids. David would always tell me who missed a lot of school because they had to be in the hospital, or how Liz would hug him in school and announce that "He is my cousin", or how the Autistic boy would be allowed to pull the fire alarm for drills so that he wasn't scared when it rang.

One day, a new boy came to school. His name was Tyler, and he had short-term memory loss. Every day I would hear how many times Tyler introduced himself to David. I think he was amused by it. Not long after, though, he came home and said "That kid Tyler, they say he can't remember stuff. But I don't agree – he always remembers my name, and when he sees me in the hall, he always yells "Hey David Thomas Dorval!"

Then Middle School came. How would these kids survive with hundreds of kids who have never met them? Dave would keep me updated on who didn't need a helper anymore, and who moved on to regular classes. Liz still hugged him in the hall. And the autistic boy? Well, "Do you know how smart he is???" he exclaimed one day. Then I would hear about the "helpers" who worked at the school to help keep it clean. These were people with Down's

Syndrome. David would get a kick out of watching them, because they would scour one trash can cover for a whole 30 minutes! The kids are in high school now. My son almost 6 feet tall and, I'm sure, wanting to be one of the "cool" guys in school. Yet, I still hear stories. There is the boy with the special crutches, and the kid in the wheelchair who will run you over if you are in his way….and another Autistic boy in his band who can look at a song once, and have the whole thing memorized….and the time he met his friend's brother, who, by the sounds of it has Tourette's. The list goes on and on.

And Liz? Well, she shares her cookies with him on the bus, and still hugs him in the hallways at school. I guess some things will never change.

Holly Dorval

Holly is married, and a mother of one. She has as Associates Degree in Accounting, and worked as a bookkeeper for over 15 years. Currently she is a stay-at-home Mom who also runs a small business out of her house.

A New Chapter in our Lives

We have watched our children grow from tiny infant, to curious toddlers, to headstrong teenagers. We attended countless parent teacher conferences, sat in on numerous Special Education meetings, and worked closely with therapists and advocates to ensure that our kids got everything they needed to succeed in life. Now they are donning their caps and gowns, getting ready to walk across a stage that will cross them over into the next phase of their lives. While we are so very proud, in the back of our mind lingers one very momentous question: Are either one of us ready for the future?

What will become of our children when they are grown? Their needs to not end simply because they have finished school. Will they be productive members of society? Who will care for them during the day? These times are fast approaching for me, and while I am uneasy on what the future may hold, I am also comforted by a story that a woman once told me about her autistic grandson.

He had lived at home after aging out of school, and when he turned 30 his parents felt that he was finally ready to live on his own. When they approached him with the opportunity, he was adamantly against it. No amount of reassurance about his capabilities would change his mind. Then one day the grandmother called her grandson and asked him why he did not want to become independent and move out of his parents house. His response was simple. He did not want to be forgotten. If he was to leave his parents home, they would surely forget about him and that was more than he could bare.

The grandmother gently assured her grandson that he would never be forgotten, for their love for him was too strong. They would still go shopping together, come together for family functions, and see one another as often as they wished. She reminded him of all their other relatives who did not live with them, yet remained a vital part of their family.

The grandson took this new knowledge and let it resonate overnight. When he woke the next morning, he announced to his parents that he was ready for his own place. Transitioning first to a group home, then to a place of his own, this boy is now thriving as an adult. The challenges were vast over the years, yet he overcame each obstacle just as any ordinary person would. He may have taken the long road, but his destination was the same regardless.

So these are not endings, but a new chapter in our lives. A time for us parents to loosen the hold on our children and release them into the world. We have nurtured their mind, their hearts, and their aspirations for years. Now it is time to sit back and watch our beautiful buds bloom before our eyes. Let them go chase their dreams and take their place on this rollercoaster that we call life.

Amy Quonce

Interested in submitting a story for the book's sequel?

Parents, caregivers, friends, teachers, coaches, and even individual themselves are encouraged to zero in on a small moment in their lives and write about it. These can be funny, inspiring, heartwarming, and yes even tear jerking...we want them all!

I have been asked in the first book if there is an age limit on who we write about or a limit on what type of disabilities the book is accepting. The answer is no...this book is for everybody. Is there a member of your community who triumphs over a physical disability? Perhaps your child has a classmate whose developmental delays causes them to have a hilarious outlook on life. Everybody knows somebody whose life has been affected in some way by a disability. All stories are welcomed!!

You can email your submissions to WindingRoadBook@aol.com.

Stay in touch by visiting www.WindingRoadBook.Weebly.Com & Facebook.com/WindingRoadBook.